MW00423491

Intelligent Guides to Wines & Top Vineyards

Alsace

Wines of Alsace

Benjamin Lewin MW

Preface

Based on my book, *Wines of France*, this Guide is devoted specifically to Alsace. The first part discusses the region and its wines; the second part has individual profiles of the top producers. The basic idea is that the first part explains the character and range of the wines, and the second part shows how each winemaker interprets that character.

In the first part I address the nature of the wines made today and ask how this has changed, how it's driven by tradition or competition, and how styles may evolve in the future. I show how the wines are related to the terroir and to the types of grape varieties that are grown, and I explain the classification system. For each region, I suggest reference wines that I believe typify the area; in some cases, where there is a split between, for example, modernists and traditionalists, there may be wines from each camp.

There's no single definition for what constitutes a top producer. Leading producers range from those who are so prominent as to represent the common public face of an appellation to those who demonstrate an unexpected potential on a tiny scale. The producers profiled in the guide should represent the best of both tradition and innovation in wine in the region

In the profiles, I have tried to give a sense of each producer's aims for his wines, of the personality and philosophy behind them— to meet the person who makes the wine, as it were, as much as to review the wines themselves. For each producer I suggest reference wines that are a good starting point for understanding his style. Most of the producers welcome visits, although some require appointments: details are in the profiles.

The guide is based on many visits to France over recent years. I owe an enormous debt to the hundreds of producers who cooperated in this venture by engaging in discussion and opening innumerable bottles for tasting. This guide would not have been possible without them.

Benjamin Lewin MW

How to read the producer profiles

The second part of this guide consists of profiles of individual wine producers. Each profile shows a sample label, a picture of the winery, and details of production, followed by a description of the producer and winemaker. The producer's rating (from one to four stars) is shown to the right of the name.

The profiles are organized geographically, and each group of profiles is preceded by a map showing the locations of starred producers to help plan itineraries.

A full list of the symbols used in the profiles appears at the start of the profile section. This is an example of a profile:

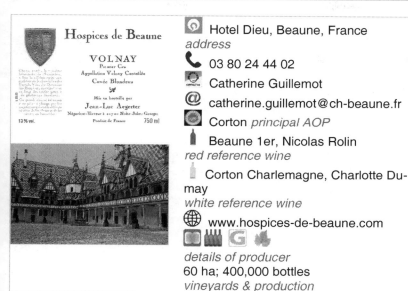

Hospices de Beaune

VOLNAY
Premier Cru
Appellation Volnay Contrôlée
Cuvée Blondeau

Mis en bouteille par
Jean-Luc Aegerter
Négociant-Éleveur à 21700 Nuits-Saint-Georges

13 % vol.   Produit de France   750 ml

🔘 Hotel Dieu, Beaune, France
address

📞 03 80 24 44 02

☎ Catherine Guillemot

@ catherine.guillemot@ch-beaune.fr

⊙ Corton *principal AOP*

🍷 Beaune 1er, Nicolas Rolin
red reference wine

🍾 Corton Charlemagne, Charlotte Dumay
white reference wine

🌐 www.hospices-de-beaune.com

details of producer
60 ha; 400,000 bottles
vineyards & production

The Hospices de Beaune was founded in 1443 by Nicolas Rolin, chancellor of Burgundy, as a hospital for the poor. Standing in the heart of Beaune, the original buildings of the Hotel Dieu, now converted into a museum, surround a courtyard where an annual auction of wines was first held in 1859. The wines come from vineyards held as part of the endowment of the Hospices, and are sold in November to negociants who then take possession of the barrels and mature the wines in their own styles. (Today the auction is held in the modern covered marketplace opposite the Hotel Dieu.) There are 45 cuvées (32 red and 13 white); most come from premier or grand crus from the Côte de Beaune or Côte de Nuits, but because holdings are small (depending on past donations of land to the Hospices) many cuvées consist of blends from different crus (and are identified by brand names). The vines are cultivated, and the wine is made, by the Hospices. For some years the vineyards of the Hospices were not tended as carefully as they might have been, and the winemaking was less than perfect, but the appointment of a new régisseur has led to improvements in the present century. The name of the Hospices is only a starting point, because each negociant stamps his own style on the barriques he buys.

Contents

Alsace

Alsace must surely have the most picturesque villages and vineyards in France. Driving along the Route des Vins from Strasbourg to Colmar, you pass through an endless series of wonderfully preserved medieval villages. This is quite surprising considering that the region has changed hands several times in wars between France and Germany. Germanic influence has impacted wine production, from the types of grape varieties to the mix of dry and sweet styles. It is no accident that Alsace is the only region in France where the focus is as much on grape varieties as appellations. Its history has also had a significant effect on aspirations to quality (or lack thereof).

You are always conscious of the Vosges mountains. Vineyards extend eastward from the lower slopes of the mountains. Most of the best vineyards are on the middle slopes between 200 and 350 m, which are a degree or so warmer than the land above or below. From the relatively narrow band of vineyards, the land opens out to the east on to a plain extending to the Rhine (which however is too far away to have any direct influence on the climate). The Vosges mountains are the dominant climatic influence. "Bad weather stops on the Vosges," they claim locally. Because rainfall is absorbed by the Vosges, Alsace had the driest vineyards in all France.

The cool climate has historically forced a concentration on white grape varieties. Today the most important varieties are Riesling and Gewürztraminer, each with about 20% of plantings; Pinot Gris is a little lower at 15%. Fifty years ago, the most important variety was the nondescript Sylvaner, which is now disappearing from view, together with the even more characterless Chasselas. The other big difference is that the trend of global warming has led Pinot Noir to increase from insignificant amounts to about 10% of plantings. Total plantings have increased from 12,000 ha in 1982 to just over 15,000 ha today.

Bad weather stops on the Vosges.

Virtually all approved vineyards in Alsace are Appellation Contrôlée. Unusually for France, the AOP is organized in terms of varietals rather than regions, and almost all wines are labeled with the name of a single grape variety. This means the wine is a monovarietal, except for Pinot Blanc. Nominally Pinot Blanc is the most commonly produced variety in Alsace, but because of a historical mix-up, wines can be called Pinot Blanc when they contain Auxerrois, a much inferior variety. Roughly two thirds of the grapevines that were classified as Pinot Blanc are really Auxerrois, so many wines labeled as Pinot Blanc actually contain a majority of Auxerrois.

The Gentil category comes from blending varieties, but it's always an entry-level wine. Besides the still wines, there is a good deal of sparkling wine, labeled under its own AOP as Crémant d'Alsace. Most often based on Pinot Blanc and Auxerrois, it is about a quarter of all production. (However, it may be significant that none of the producers I visited in Alsace thought it was worth including Crémant in what were often very long tastings.)

Grown since the fifteenth century, Riesling is an old variety in Alsace. Gewürztraminer and Muscat date from a century later. Pinot Gris was probably first grown in Alsace in the seventeenth century: it

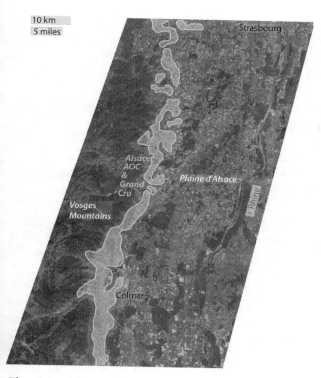

The vineyards in AOP Alsace form a band parallel with the Vosges mountains running from Strasbourg to south of Colmar. To the east of the vineyards, the Plaine d'Alsace extends for about 20 km to the Rhine.

used to be called Tokay d'Alsace, reflecting the (improbable) legend that it was brought from Hungary, but European Community rules now ban use of this name because of supposed confusion with Tokaji.

Alsace's reputation for quality wines is a feature of the past half century. The wines used to be regarded as low quality, mass production—what the French call vins de comptoir. One story dates this reputation from the period when Alsace came under German control following the war of 1870, and production was used to improve German wines. But in fact, Alsace had 65,000 hectares of vineyards (five times today's plantings!) mostly given over to high-yielding, low quality grape varieties when the war started. Nor did production habits change when Alsace became French again after the First World War. Quality varieties began a slow takeover after the AOP finally came into full effect in 1962, but it was not until 1980 that the last low-grade varieties were legally excluded.

In spite of the move to quality, Alsace has been undergoing an identity crisis for years. There is a great difference between the cheap wines produced by most negociants or cooperatives and the quality wines produced by independent growers (and by some producers who have vineyards but also buy grapes). A major problem is that yields are far too high; while good producers will be well below the legal limits, there is no obligation. There is no agreement on style, so that wines that are not specifically identified as late harvest may in fact range from absolutely bone-dry to off-dry or even relatively sweet. All of this is a consequence of the looseness of regulations and the classification system.

Yields have been reduced only slowly from the bad old days, from a maximum of 120 hl/ha in 1974, to 96 hl/ha in 1982, to 80 hl/ha today. Limiting yields for individual varieties (as opposed to total production in the vineyard) became the rule only in 1999 (until then, the average for any vineyard/grower had to conform to the limit, but one variety could be above and another below it). Maximum yields are much higher than allowed elsewhere in France; only Champagne is higher. Yield limits are the same for all grape varieties. It is obvious that quality would be improved by restricting yields, but "the large negociants and cooperatives are against it," explains Céline Meyer of Domaine Josmeyer. Independent growers are in a small minority.

The appellation system in Alsace is unique in France. There are only two levels of appellation for still wines: AOP Alsace, and AOP Alsace Grand Cru (the grand cru is named on the label). The 52 grand crus were created over a protracted period: Schlossberg was the first in 1975, then a large group followed in 1983, and another group in 1992. They cover 7% of the vineyard area and account for 5% of production, as yields are lower (originally 70 hl/ha but reduced to 55 hl/ha in 2001). Terroirs vary widely. The common feature is elevation: all are on the slopes of the Vosges, sometimes

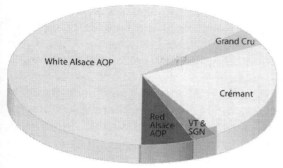

The great majority of Alsace production is white Alsace AOP. Crémant is the second major category. Red Alsace has become significant. Grand Cru and VT/SGN remain small categories.

quite steep, often rising up sharply from a town. Grand crus are restricted to Riesling, Gewürztraminer, Pinot Gris, and Muscat (actually there is very little of the last). (Other varieties, such as Pinot Noir, can be planted, but cannot be labeled as Grand Cru.)

There are special regulations for sweet dessert wines. Wines from berries with more than a certain sugar level can be labeled as Vendange Tardive (late harvest), and may have some botrytis. At higher sugar levels, Selection des Grains Nobles comes exclusively from botrytized grapes. Both VT and SGN are restricted to the same four varieties as the grand crus.

The Grape Varieties

The best grape varieties of Alsace are distinctly aromatic. The lesser varieties of Chasselas and Sylvaner make pleasant wines for summer quaffing but rarely have much interest. Occasionally you find an old vines cuvée, where lowered yields have brought some character; usually this takes the form of more savory, herbal impressions: interesting in their own way for showing a different potential of the variety, but not rising to the level of the noble varieties.

Pinot Blanc might make an interesting wine, but as it is usually mostly Auxerrois, it tends to lack flavor interest. In fact, I am not sure I have encountered a single Pinot Blanc in Alsace that was made exclusively from the named variety. I did find some monovarietal Auxerrois, with vieilles vignes cuvées from Josmeyer and Paul Blanck really demonstrating an unusual level of character.

Chardonnay is permitted in Alsace for the sparkling Crémant, but not for still wine. "Few people can see the difference between an Auxerrois vine and a Chardonnay; quite a few growers use some Chardonnay in their still Pinot Blanc blends, but would never admit doing it. It always goes officially into the Crémant," says Olivier Humbrecht MW of Zind-Humbrecht. So the composition and quality of "Pinot Blanc" are rather unpredictable. "Chardonnay was not admitted in the AOC category, mostly for political reasons, I think, not quality," says Olivier, whose "Zind" cuvée (a Vin de France) gives a good indication of what Chardonnay can achieve in Alsace. Coming from the top Windsbuhl vineyard, it shows the character of terroir as much as the variety.

Muscat can in principle be intensely grapey, but is a mixed bag in Alsace as there are plantings of both Muscat Blanc à Petit Grains (high quality) and Muscat Ottonel (much lower quality). Alsace's quality wines therefore come from Pinot Gris, Gewürztraminer, and Riesling.

Pinot Gris reaches its full height of expression in Alsace; certainly it bears no resemblance at all to Pinot Grigio, the expression of the same variety in Italy. It's grown scarcely anywhere else in France. Although it is a color variant of Pinot Noir, with skin of varying color, it is vinified as a white wine and its aromatic profile is different. I wouldn't go so far as to call its character blowsy, but it has relatively low acidity, and with some rare exceptions, tends to have broad, soft flavors, sometimes with an oily texture, showing stone fruits tending to apricots; but it can also move in a more savory direction, sometimes veering towards suggestions of mushrooms.

The big issue with Pinot Gris is that it really reaches ripeness only at high alcohol levels, so usually fermentation stops before completion, leaving some residual sugar. "It's complicated to make a dry Pinot Gris," is the way Céline Meyer at Domaine Josmeyer puts it. Residual sugar may be fairly minimal for wines labeled as Alsace AOP, but most grand cru Pinot Gris is perceptibly sweet. It also makes a fine late harvest wine, where those notes of mushrooms, accentuated by botrytis, can add complexity to the sweet apricot fruits.

Gewürz is German for spice, but Gewürztraminer is usually more perfumed than spicy. It is by far the most aromatic variety of

Vinification traditionally takes place in foudres.

Alsace, with a typical scent of roses on the nose; lychee fruits are characteristic on the palate. The classic description of Gewürztraminer is that it smells sweet but tastes dry, although this is not really true in Alsace. Those aromas of roses can turn quite phenolic on the finish and give a drying impression, but usually there is enough residual sugar to show perceptible sweetness. Even with some residual sugar, the alcohol level is often quite high. Gewürztraminer is a mainstay of the late harvest wines, with peaches and apricots joining lychees in Vendange Tardive, and botrytized flavors hiding the usual perfume at the level of Selection de Grains Nobles.

Riesling is the glory of Alsace, appearing in all styles from completely dry to totally botrytized. None of the other varieties can compete with its purity of flavors. When completely dry it can be steely and mineral, sometimes even saline. Fruits remain in the citrus spectrum, sometimes overlaid by a characteristic touch of petrol

Reference Wines for Dry White Alsace	
Chardonnay (Vin de France)	*Zind-Humbrecht, Zind*
Sylvaner	*Paul Blanck, Vieilles Vignes*
Auxerrois	*Josmeyer, "H" Vieilles Vignes*
Pinot Blanc	*Marc Tempé, Zellenberg*
Muscat	*Domaine Ostertag, Fronholz* *Domaine Weinbach*
Pinot Gris	*Bott-Geyl* *Josmeyer, La Fromenteau* *Louis Sipp, Trottacker*
Gewürztraminer	*Paul Blanck* *Bott-Geyl* *Louis Sipp*
Riesling	*Valentin Zusslin, Liebenberg* *Meyer Fonné, Pfoeller* *Marc Tempé, Grafenreben* *Louis Sipp, Hagel* *Domaine Josmeyer, Le Kottabe* *Domaine Paul Blanck, Rosenbourg*

(which develops earlier here than it does in Germany). Riesling offers producers more of a choice in determining style, because it ripens at lower alcohol levels than Pinot Gris or Gewürztraminer. Because Riesling ripens more slowly, it is less prominent among the late harvest styles than Pinot Gris or Gewürztraminer.

Virtually all high quality wine in Alsace is monovarietal. Marcel Deiss is probably the only producer who blends his top wines. When I asked Jean-Michel Deiss if he uses all seven varieties of Alsace he said, "Yes, all thirteen varieties!" There are the principal varieties such as Riesling (more than half of his plantings), then some secondary varieties (about a third), and finally, less than 10%, there are some old varieties that he is trying to preserve from disappearing. Jean-Michel is quick to point out that he does not produce his wines by assemblage, the mixing of wines made from different varieties, but each is a single wine produced from grapes of different varieties intermingled in the vineyard. "I don't make wines to express the cépage but to express the terroir," he says. He believes that to express terroir you need to grow varieties together. But this is distinctly a minority view.

Because the emphasis in Alsace is on aromatic varieties, there is no malolactic fermentation, which would introduce creamy notes clashing with varietal character (as well as reducing acidity in Pinot Gris and Gewürztraminer, which are already low acid varieties). So alcoholic fermentation is followed directly by a period of maturation. Fermentation in the traditional foudres is still used for top wines, but these days most wines are fermented in temperature-controlled stainless steel. Maturation usually lasts a few months for entry level wines; top wines are most often bottled just before the next harvest. "In Burgundy they talk about négociant-éleveurs but they don't exist in Alsace because we don't have élevage," says Marc Tempé, who is one of the few producers to break with tradition and use extended élevage in barriques. With rare exceptions, protracted maturation is not part of the style in Alsace.

The only black grape permitted in Alsace is Pinot Noir. Until recently, this was very definitely an also-ran, with most of the wines showing a resemblance to rosé. Global warming has changed things: producers are now taking red wine seriously. Have you always made Pinot Noir, I asked Étienne Sipp of Domaine Louis Sipp. "Yes but not in the present way. There is a big change, people are rethinking Pinot Noir, they plant it in good places, they produce more concentrated wine." It's a sign how things have changed that at Hugel, who were probably first to make Pinot Noir in a Burgundian way when they started in 1977, winemaker Johnny Hugel said "If you force me to make Pinot Noir, I'll make vinegar," but today Marc Hugel makes very fine Pinot Noir.

Grand Crus in Alsace are often the most elevated sites near each village. Kitterlé rises up steeply immediately above the town of Guebwiller.

"The idea is not to copy Burgundy, but the Pinot comes from the most calcareous places in the vineyards. We want to produce something silky and elegant in Pinot Noir," says Jean-Christophe Bott of Domaine Bott-Geyl. The style in Alsace usually more resembles Côte de Beaune than Côte de Nuits, and tends to be soft, smooth, and earthy. The reds sometimes seem to show an aromatic spectrum relating to the fact that Alsace focuses on aromatic white varieties. The best wines tend to come from calcareous areas of grand crus. Typically they are ready about five or six years after the vintage, but will hold as long again. The warming trend has definitely created a new opportunity for Alsace. "With the climate change, we probably now have the same climate in Alsace that Burgundy had twenty years ago," said Étienne Hugel. It's an interesting question as to whether this will be recognized by allowing Pinot Noir to be included in the grand cru classification.

Reference Wines for Pinot Noir	
Burlenberg	*Marcel Deiss*
Les Neveux (lieu-dit Pflostig)	*Maison Hugel*
"V" (Vorbourg grand cru)	*René Muré*
"M" (Mambourg grand cru)	*Marc Tempé*
"W" (Clos des Capucins)	*Domaine Weinbach*
Bollenberg Harmonie	*Valentin Zusslin*

The Grand Crus

With only two categories, Alsace AOP and Alsace Grand Cru, the appellation system in Alsace is one of the least informative in France. Grand Crus were controversial when they were introduced, and they remain controversial today. The lack of any hierarchy in the initial classification system—all AOP wines were originally described simply as Vins d'Alsace—led to the establishment of a committee in the 1970s to consider the promotion of the best vineyards to higher status. But the results were so controversial that several of the most important producers refuse to use the system. The basic problem was that in order to get the system approved, too many grand crus were created, and many of them are much too large. The first one set the pattern. The hill of Schlossberg lies between the great château of Kaysersberg and the town of Kintzheim, avowedly including some of the best terroir in Alsace. The original committee recommended it should include a total area of about 25 ha, but as finally approved it consists of about 80 ha: politics triumphed over geology.

It is no coincidence that most of the villages on the Route des Vins have a single grand cru associated with them. Each village proposed its best vineyards for grand cru status, and some sort of liberté, égalité, fraternité resulted, with most villages getting one, and only one, grand cru. Often enough, it's the steepest hill near the village. It's fair to say that the grand crus do include most of the best sites in Alsace, but the political nature of the process makes the label unreliable as an indication of the very best quality. "Johnny Hugel (who

*Grand Cru Schoenen-
bourg rises up
immediately outside the
town walls of Ri-
quewihr.*

chaired the first committee) wanted to define the best of the best, but
his peers didn't understand that there would be problems years later
if you expanded the grand crus," says Marc Hugel. The Hugels believe that the whole concept has been devalued, and so far have
refused to use the names of grand crus.

"There are too many grand crus in Alsace, and the size of some
of them is just too big. Also the yields in grand crus are too high.
More than half of grand cru juice goes to cooperatives, who have no
idea what to do with it, so you can find grand cru wines in super-
markets at (low) prices that are simply criminal," says Hubert
Trimbach. The most notable example of a wine from a top site that
does not state the grand cru on the label is in fact Trimbach's Clos

Ste. Hune, widely acknowledged to be one of the best, in fact probably the best, Riesling from Alsace, which comes from a 1.6 ha vineyard in the Rosacker Grand Cru. As Hubert points out dryly, "Clos Ste. Hune and even Frédéric Emile (another top cuvée from Trimbach) are better known than any grand cru." But by the time you add up the top wines from Trimbach, Hugel (the major owner of the grand crus Sporen and Schoenenbourg), and Léon Beyer (another top producer who does not use the grand cru system), a significant proportion of grand crus have been deprived of recognition.

"It's not the number of grand crus that's the issue but the delimitation. Some of the tops and bottoms of hills should perhaps be premier cru," says Felix Meyer at Meyer-Fonné. Premier cru is the name of the game in Alsace today, with a proposal at INAO to create a more hierarchical appellation structure, including premier crus and perhaps village wines. This development is already widely anticipated, with many producers labeling single vineyard wines with the names of lieu-dits that they hope will become premier crus; some producers are labeling wines from plots around each village with its name. But this will not eliminate a surreal element in the present system. "Some premier cru wines may sell at higher prices than some grand cru wines," says Céline Meyer at Domaine Josmeyer, recognizing that lieu-dits are used to indicate wines of higher quality, whereas grand crus remain extremely variable. Could any grand crus be demoted? "No, there is no willingness to open the grand cru box. The system is not perfect but it exists. It's much more important to organize a classification of the intermediate levels," says Étienne Sipp at Domaine Louis Sipp.

With several hundred lieu-dits being considered for promotion, it's a legitimate concern whether the system will become so complicated as to confuse the consumer. In any case, nothing seems likely to happen soon—producers are talking in terms of the next ten years or so. I am afraid that the system will lack credibility unless the variability of the grand crus is taken in hand at the same time. But it seems likely that the most that will happen is more precise definition of which specific varieties are allowed in each grand cru. This may bring a recognition of the significant advances made with red wine by adding Pinot Noir to the permitted list for some grand crus.

Grand Cru Sommerberg is just outside Niedermorschwihr.

Grand crus are better known for extra richness and (sometimes) for higher quality than for specific aspects of terroir. Yet there is a wide range of terroirs, including granite, volcanic, sandstone, marl, and calcareous. Among the granite grand crus, Brand is taut, Furstentum is delicate, Schlossberg gives precision, and Sommerberg has grip. The calcareous terroir of Osterberg is upright. The marl of Geisberg and Sporen tends to opulence, and in Hengst to power. Rosacker's muschelkalk gives tension. But few grand crus have really achieved reputations in their own right, perhaps because many are associated with a single wine from a particular producer, rather than from several producers. "It's important that a lieu-dit or premier cru should be represented by multiple producers so it doesn't just have one style," says Jean-Christophe Bott.

The Sweetness of Alsace

The warming climate has resulted in a trend to leaving some residual sugar in the wine. Indeed, sugar is the word that cannot speak its name in Alsace. Wine production is bedeviled by the issue of sweetness, and the major single factor that has held Alsace back from better success in the market is probably the unpredictable level of sweetness in its wines. "When I started 35 years ago, almost all wines had less than 3 grams residual sugar. Now most wines have more. I think there is a relation between the fact that Alsace has placed itself with sweet wines and the fact that prices have stayed low. One problem is that every other region has regulations for alcohol levels and

Reference Wines for Alsace Grand Cru Riesling	
Brand	Josmeyer
Eichberg	"R" de Beyer
Furstentum	Paul Blanck
Geisberg	Trimbach
Hengst	Josmeyer
Kirchberg de Ribeauvillé	Louis Sipp
Kitterlé	Domaine Schlumberger
Mandelberg	Bott-Geyl
Muenchberg	Domaine Ostertag
Osterberg	Louis Sipp
Pfersigberg	Léon Beyer, Comtes d'Eguisheim
Pfingstberg	Valentin Zusslin
Rangen	Zind-Humbrecht
Rosacker	Trimbach, Clos St. Hune
Schlossberg	Domaine Weinbach, Cuvée St. Catherine
Schoenenbourg	Hugel, Jubilee
Sommerberg	Paul Blanck
Wineck-Schlossberg	Meyer-Fonné
Vorbourg	René Muré, Clos St. Landelin
Geisberg/Osterberg	Trimbach, Frédéric Emile

sweetness but Alsace does not," says Marc Hugel. "Our image as a dry-wine region is at risk," says Étienne Hugel.

There are two conflicting trends in Alsace today. One is a demand for dry wines to go with food; younger producers especially are trying to make wines in a drier style than their parents. The other is that sugar levels at harvest have been pushed up by warmer vintages to a point at which producers feel that alcohol would be too high if fermentation went to completion, and that it's better to have lower alcohol by leaving a little residual sugar. Even producers who consider that sweetness is a problem concede that there are benefits. "I would say that in Alsace global warming has increased enormously the quality of the wine, even if it has brought the problem of residual sugar," Marc Hugel allows. Sometimes there are suspicions that producers are stopping fermentation to make the wines more crowd-pleasing, but Jean Boxler at Domaine Albert Boxler says that, "We have more problems in continuing fermentation than in stopping it at a specific sweetness."

Some producers believe that wine should always be dry. "Our wine is bone-dry and therefore suitable to accompany food," says Hubert Trimbach. Other notable houses in this camp are Hugel and Josmeyer. But what is dry? A wine will always taste dry if it has less than 4 g/l residual sugar (this is the usual limit for calling a wine dry in most regions), but it may taste virtually dry if it has high enough acidity, even if it is over 4 g/l residual sugar.

Achieving a dry balance is more problematic with Pinot Gris and Gewürztraminer than with Riesling. Statistically speaking, if you select a Riesling from Alsace from an unknown producer you have a good chance of it being dry or almost dry, but Pinot Gris or Gewürztraminer will almost always be at least a little sweet. This is partly because these varieties reach phenolic ripeness only at higher sugar levels, and partly because they have lower acidity that makes any residual sugar more obvious.

The issue of sweetness is tied up with the grand cru system, because the grand crus were defined at a time when getting to ripeness was problematic. So they are the sites that achieve greatest ripeness, often south-facing hillsides. An outdated regulation requires potential alcohol to reach 10% at harvest, but today it's more of a problem to restrain alcohol. In a typical vintage when the grand crus were defined, the distinction might have been that a grand cru reached an acceptable level of alcohol naturally, whereas an AOC Alsace vineyard needed chaptalization. So the wines would have the same (dry) style, but the grand cru would display the extra character that goes with greater ripeness. In the present era of warmer vintages, however, the appellation vineyard may reach an acceptable level of potential alcohol, and the grand cru may rise above it. This explains why at many producers the entry level wine is always fermented to dryness, but the grand crus show some residual sugar.

The argument is basically that something has to give: either alcohol will be too high or there will be residual sugar. This might not be so much of an issue if the style was consistent for any given producer and stayed the same between vintages. Vintage variation is a problem when a wine is dry in one vintage and sweet in another. And it's equally confusing when a producer changes style from AOC Alsace to grand cru. "The problem is not with the entry level, it's more with the grand crus, where the Riesling may be picked at 14% potential alcohol. It's more difficult to achieve dry Riesling and we can find grand crus with 7-8 g/l sugar or more; it's totally stupid for the grand crus to have residual sugar," says Pierre Trimbach. In my view, this is spot on as a criticism, because it is impossible to appreciate the difference between an appellation Riesling and a grand cru Riesling if the first is dry and the second is sweet. I should admit to a prejudice here that you can't really appreciate nuances of terroir when the palate is muddied by residual sugar. So at some producers, the most interesting wines are the middle of the range, because the basic wines are too simple, but the grand crus are too sweet.

Even the most committed producers admit that it's mostly impossible (and maybe undesirable) to get completely dry Pinot Gris or Gewürztraminer from grand crus. "Pinot Gris ripens very rapidly. Sometimes you say you harvest in the morning and it's dry, you harvest in the afternoon and it's sweet," says Étienne Sipp. "Gewürztraminer will reach 13-14% when Riesling gets to 11%," Marc Hugel says, conceding, "It's better to have 14% alcohol and 7 g/l sugar than 15% alcohol and bone dry." And Céline Meyer at Domaine Josmeyer points out that "If Gewürztraminer is completely dry it's not agreeable because it's too bitter." So the consensus is that, faute de mieux, Gewürztraminer (and Pinot Gris) are going to have some sugar. "I prefer to make dry wines and for Riesling it's easy to be dry, but with the grand crus for Pinot Gris and Gewürztraminer

Reference Wines for Pinot Gris and Gewürztraminer Grand Cru and Late Harvest	
Pinot Gris	
Grand Cru	*Josmeyer, Brand*
Vendange Tardive	*Marc Kreydenweiss, Muenchberg* *Zind-Humbrecht, Clos Windsbuhl*
SGN	*Bott-Geyl, Sonnenglanz*
Gewürztraminer	
Grand Cru	*Trimbach, Cuvée des Seigneurs de Ribeaupierre*
Vendange Tardive	*Marc Tempé, Mambourg* *Domaine Weinbach, Furstentum*
SGN	*Meyer-Fonné, Sporen*

we cannot produce dry wines. To follow what the terroir has to give you, the wine would not be balanced if you picked early enough to make dry wine," says Jean-Christophe Bott. But he adds ruefully, "Of course the market is looking for dry wine." The best you can do with Pinot Gris and Gewürztraminer is usually to produce a wine that tastes very nearly dry.

Alongside the issue of sugar, is the question of botrytis. While botrytis is desirable in late harvest wines, producers differ on whether they welcome it in dry (or nearly dry) wines, but it's not uncommon, especially at the grand cru level, to have a small proportion of botrytized grapes. Indeed, at Meyer Fonné, Felix Meyer only makes SGN where there's enough botrytis not to deprive the grand cru: "In most years there's 15% or so in the grand cru Gewürztraminer, and I don't want to take that out, it's part of the character," he says. At Domaine Paul Blanck, Frédéric Blanck takes a different view: "I don't want to see botrytis in the classic (entry-level) range because it changes the flavor of everything. Botrytis is perfect in late harvest but has nothing to do with grand cru because you can get concentration without it, and we want to see the purity." You can make delicious wine with or without botrytis; it's really a matter of whether you regard it as a feature of terroir or as a complication.

Two scales coming into common use on Alsace back labels rate sweetness by 5 or 9 points. The first three points usually indicate dry, off-dry, and medium sweet.

One of the biggest problems for the consumer has been the failure to come to terms with sugar levels: unless a wine is Vendange Tardive or SGN, there is no official way to know whether it is dry or off-dry. Producers have finally realized that this is a major impediment in the marketplace, and many have introduced a scale of sweetness on the back label. Étienne Hugel was against the idea because "it means we have lost the battle," and it's fair to say that it may help to resolve uncertainty, but at the cost of reinforcing the image that wine from Alsace is not reliably dry. However, it is no more than a partial solution, because information on the back label is not evident on, for example, a restaurant wine list; and furthermore the scale is neither consistent nor objective. Some producers use a 5 point scale, some use a 9 point scale.

Actually, I do not think either scale has much significance beyond the first three points, because once a wine is sweet, it is sweet, and it would be a rare person who would choose it on the basis of just how sweet. The critical point is whether a wine tastes bone dry, or what I call ambiguously dry (when you don't think it's bone dry, but can't quite taste sweetness), or distinctly off-dry. Aside from that, the problem is that right at the most sensitive point of the scale, the difference between bone-dry and off-dry, most producers are assigning #1 or #2 on the basis of taste. This is a mistake because sensitivities differ: indeed, when I've questioned whether a particular wine should really be #1, producers sometimes say that the number depends on who is making the assignment that day. "The problem is that everyone has their own system, when I see what's on the label sometimes I'm astonished," says Marc Hugel. None of this is going to work until producers accept that there is an international standard for bone-dry wine: less than 4 g/l of residual sugar. The best solution of all, of course, would be for Alsace to have a formal AOP of Alsace Sec that appears on the front label for wine that is unambiguously dry. If even in Champagne they have started to put dosage levels on the label, why can't they put the level of residual sugar on the label in Alsace?

For all of the problems with sugar confusing the palate of sup-posedly dry wines, there is no argument about the quality of the sweet wines of Alsace. Vendange Tardive and Selection de Grains Nobles dessert wines have been classified separately in Alsace since 1984. Even here the classification refers to the sugar level at time of harvest rather than to residual sugar after fermentation; however, given the sugar levels at harvest, VT and SGN wines are always sweet. Chaptalization cannot be used for VT or SGN wines; in fact, the regulations for their production are among the strictest in France for dessert wines. Their reputation is as high as for any sweet wine anywhere, but they represent only an average 1-2% of production, with amounts fluctuating widely from year to year according to vin-tage conditions.

"We cannot compete on price or varietal name. We are on steep slopes, we have high labor costs. Let's try to put our terroir into the bottle," says Étienne Sipp, expressing his view of the future for Al-sace. The region has one of the great varieties in Riesling, which I think is possibly the most versatile white variety of all. There is a se-ries of different terroirs at grand cru level where Riesling shows all the nuances of its range of expression as a dry wine. Pinot Gris and Gewürztraminer can show real varietal character in Alsace. The late harvest wines can achieve great purity and interest extending beyond mere sweetness. It is a shame that uncertainty about wine styles, and failure to be strict enough about yields and to take the classification system in hand, have prevented the region from establishing the reputation it deserves.

Vintages

Historically Alsace has alternated between good vintages and poor vintages, but the recent global warming trend has produced a run of good vintages, albeit with different characters. There's a marked difference between 2007 or 2009, which are both overtly rich, and 2010, which has high acidity, for example, providing a style for every taste.

2015	Warm, dry season gave low yields, dry wines are low in acidity, there are late harvest wines, and good Pinot Noir.
2014	Cool August produced restrained dry whites with high acid and few late harvest wines.
2013	Rain at harvest meant that early pickers did best, so the wines tend to be light and fresh. This is a vintage for early drinking.
2012	Warm August and cool September gave good results, with a classic balance of fruit to acidity. It was especially successful for Pinot Noir.
2011	Decent but not great vintage, generally giving a fresh, fruity style; not much in the way of late harvest wines. Dry wines should be drunk early.
2010	Very high acidity caused many wines to take time to come around. Riesling can still be piercing, but the best wines are fresh and pure with classic minerality, and should have longevity. There are few late harvest wines.
2009	Precocious vintage in rich style, with powerful Rieslings and opulent Pinot Gris and Gewürztraminer. Alcohol is high for dry wines.
2008	Generally cool season saved by Indian summer; the style is often restrained, and some wines were slow to open. Not as good as 2007 or 2009.
2007	Regarded as a great vintage all round, rich with even Riesling tending to opulence rather than minerality. Possibly the richest since 1997, with some great botrytized wines.

2006	A variable year, with rather heterogeneous results resulting from difficulties with getting to ripeness, but good acidity for Rieslings.
2005	Not such a good year in Alsace as elsewhere in France, with some problems reaching ripeness; grand crus are the most reliable.
2004	High yields resulted in lack of concentration. Rieslings performed best. There are few late harvest wines.
2003	The great heat of this vintage produced wines that matured early, although some of the reds have been very fine.
2002	Difficult year because of alternating hot and cold conditions, but the best wines had good structure and acidity, and sufficient ripeness.
2001	Poor and late start to season, recovery in August, then problems in September, but wines were harvested in October Indian summer, giving some exceptionally fine late harvest wines.
2000	An early start was followed by a favorable growing season, but there were heavy rains in October. Dry wines are good, if not outstanding, and there are even some late harvest wines.

Profiles of Estates

Ratings

*** Excellent producers defining the very best of the appellation

** Top producers whose wines typify the appellation

* Very good producers making wines of character that rarely disappoint

Symbols

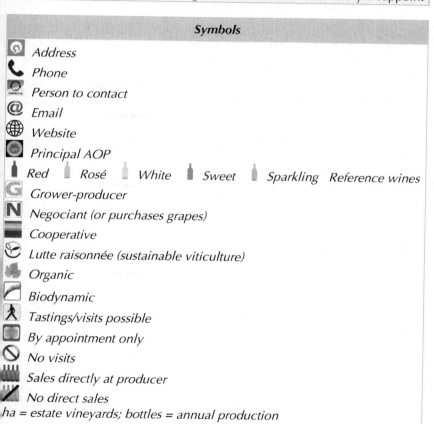

Address

Phone

Person to contact

Email

Website

Principal AOP

Red   Rosé   White   Sweet   Sparkling Reference wines

Grower-producer

Negociant (or purchases grapes)

Cooperative

Lutte raisonnée (sustainable viticulture)

Organic

Biodynamic

Tastings/visits possible

By appointment only

No visits

Sales directly at producer

No direct sales

ha = estate vineyards; bottles = annual production

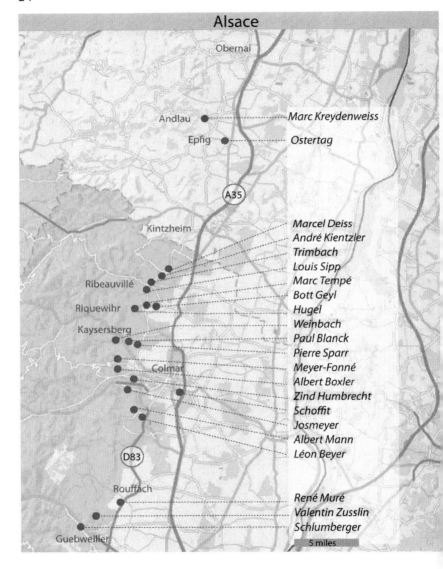

Alsace

Obernai

Andlau •---------------------- Marc Kreydenweiss

Epfig •----------------- Ostertag

A35

Kintzheim   Marcel Deiss
                                   André Kientzler
                                   Trimbach
                                   Louis Sipp
Ribeauvillé   Marc Tempé
                                   Bott Geyl
Riquewihr •   Hugel
                                   Weinbach
Kaysersberg   Paul Blanck
                                   Pierre Sparr
              Colmar   Meyer-Fonné
                                   Albert Boxler
                                   Zind Humbrecht
                                   Schoffit
                                   Josmeyer
                                   Albert Mann
D83   Léon Beyer

Rouffach
                                   René Muré
                                   Valentin Zusslin
                                   Schlumberger
Guebweiller   5 miles

Domaine Léon Beyer **

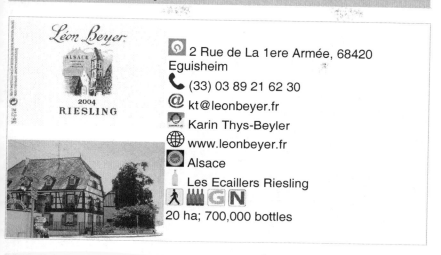

2 Rue de La 1ere Armée, 68420 Eguisheim

📞 (33) 03 89 21 62 30

@ kt@leonbeyer.fr

Karin Thys-Beyler

🌐 www.leonbeyer.fr

Alsace

Les Ecaillers Riesling

20 ha; 700,000 bottles

This is one of the most traditional houses in Alsace—"Viticulteurs de Père en Fils depuis 1580"—formally founded in 1867. Vineyards, including an additional 40 ha that the Beyers work but do not own, are in the vicinity of Eguisheim. All of Alsace's varieties are represented, although Sylvaner is not being replanted. Beyer takes pride in making wines to accompany food, which means that everything is vinified bone dry (except for Vendange Tardive or SGN). "Typical and classic Alsace wines are, and always have been, dry, fresh and light." Vinification is in very old foudres, and the wine spends eight months on the lees, but vintages are often released somewhat later than other producers. Marc Beyer says that, "The style of the house has not changed in the past fifty years, except that yields have decreased so concentration has increased." The dry wines fall into three ranges: Classic, Reserves, and Grandes Cuvées. As Marc Beyer is one of the strongest critics of the grand cru system, Beyer's own names are used for the Grandes Cuvées, although the Riesling Les Ecaillers comes from the grand cru Pfersigberg, and the Riesling R de Beyer is from grand cru Eichberg. The top wines carry the label Comte d'Eguisheim, and are made only in the best years. They include Pinot Gris and Gewürztraminer, as well as Riesling, again from grand cru vineyards. They age well: the Riesling 2000 was vibrant and lively in 2014. Beyer also produces several Eaux de Vies.

Domaine Paul Blanck

32 Grand-Rue, 68240 Kientzheim, Alsace

(33) 03 89 78 23 56

info@blanck.com

Philippe Blanck

www.blanck.com

Alsace

Schlossberg Riesling

36 ha; 230,000 bottles

"My grandfather Paul established the domain in the 1920s, but we are the nineteenth generation of growers in the village, although there's nothing special about that," says Philippe Blanck, who runs the domain today with his cousin Frédéric, the winemaker. Vineyards are local: "The idea is to work the vineyards around the valley of Kaysersberg, it's interesting because we have many different types of soil here," Philippe explains. The range of dry wines is divided between the Classic Cuvées and Vins de Terroir. About 60% of production, the Classic Cuvées include all the varietals, and are vinified dry, or almost dry, in stainless steel, and bottled under screwcap. The Vins de Terroir come from lieu-dits or grand crus. After fermentation in stainless steel, they mature for twelve months in foudres. Here the natural richness is expressed by allowing some residual sugar. "The people who buy the Vins de Terroir know the wines so they aren't confused by varying sweetness," Philippe says. The style tends generally to richness, even at the Classic level, where there is often a buttery undercurrent. The range includes an impressive array of seven grand crus, with six in Riesling, and three each in Pinot Gris or Gewürztraminer. Riesling varies from the delicacy of Furstentum to the richness of Wineck-Schlossberg, and the sheer grip of Sommerberg. Pinot Gris and Gewürztraminer show great character, often with a lovely savory or herbal counterpoise to the typical sweetness.

Domaine Bott-Geyl ★★

📍 1 rue du Petit Château, 68980 Beblenheim

📞 (33) 03 89 47 90 04

@ info@bott-geyl.com

👤 Jean-Christophe Bott & Valérie Bott-Geyl

🌐 www.bott-geyl.com

🔴 Alsace

🍾 Grafenreben Riesling

22 ha; 85,000 bottles

Located in a back street of Beblenheim, surrounded by suburban housing, the building is much larger than it appears from the outside, as a new three storey warehouse-like gravity-feed winery was constructed three years ago on top of the old caves. Vinification is in a mix of stainless steel and old foudres; most cuvées have some of each. The key to the style here is that fermentation is very slow, lasting several months, so the wines are bottled in the summer following the vintage, as by then there has been ample extraction. Jean-Christophe Bott doesn't have a set idea about style: "Each vintage imprints its character," he says. Although he tries to pick early, he believes the balance may differ with the vintage, so the wines are not necessarily dry. Christophe's aim of producing dry wines is usually achieved with Riesling, but balance in Pinot Gris and Gewürztraminer generally requires some residual sugar. The wines are divided into Vins d'Assemblage (blends of varieties), Vins de Fruits (Les Eléments: Riesling, Muscat, Pinot Gris, and Gewürztraminer), and the Vins de Terroir (lieu-dits and grand crus); and then of course the sweet wines. By the time you reach the vins de terroir, most of the wines do in fact have a touch of residual sugar. The style here often has a delicious sweet-sour balance, with savory impressions counterpoised with the fruits. It's always measured, so that Pinot Gris and Gewürztraminer show their character without overwhelming.

Domaine Albert Boxler

**

📍 78 Rue Trois Epis, Niedermorschwihr, 68230

📞 +33 (0)3 89 27 11 07

@ albert.boxler@9online.fr

👤 Jean Boxler

🟢 Alsace

🍾 Brand, Riesling

14 ha; 60,000 bottles

Discretely located in the main street of the town (no sign is evident in the street, but when you go round the back the winery and the family house are organized around a charming courtyard in typical Alsace style), the domain is just under the grand cru of Sommerberg. This is very much a family domain; I tasted with Jean Boxler in the house, with children playing in the next room. Boxlers have been here since the seventeenth century, but the domain was created by Albert Boxler in 1946 when he started to bottle his own wine. His grandson Jean has been making the wine since 1996. Most of the 30 individual vineyard parcels are in the immediate neighborhood, including several that are used to make different cuvées from Sommerberg. All of the cépages are grown here, but the focus is on Riesling, which is 40% of plantings. Everything is vinified as whole cluster, and there's a tendency to vinify the sweet wines in stainless steel and the dry wines in oak, but it doesn't always exactly work out. The Riesling is usually dry, but the Pinot Gris is usually demi-sec. Jean is not a fanatic about dryness and believes that the overall balance is more important. A pleasing sense of restraint characterizes all Albert Boxler's wines. Contrasting with the natural acidity there is a common warm softness. A consistent style runs across cépages, intensifying in Riesling, and then from Alsace to Grand Cru to Vieilles Vignes Grand Cru. Even the Crémant shows precision.

Engelgarten

Domaine Marcel Deiss ★★

15 route du Vin, 68750 Bergheim
(33) 03 89 73 63 37
marceldeiss@marceldeiss.com
Matthieu Deiss
www.marceldeiss.com
Alsace
Rotenberg Riesling

27 ha; 135,000 bottles

My last discussion with Jean-Michel Deiss had a surreal air. I found him doing the pigeage, physically immersed in a cuve of Pinot. I had to perch on top of a ladder leaning against the vat to talk with the disembodied head of Jean-Michel as he wallowed in the must. Jean-Michel has the air of a fanatic. "Cépage is a nonsense, it's a modern concept. It's impossible to make a great wine from a single cépage," he says. But he is a fanatic for making wine true to what he sees as the ancient tradition of Alsace: from more than one variety rather than from a single cépage. He is quick to point out that he does not produce his wines by assemblage, the mixing of wines made from different varieties, but each wine is produced from grapes of different varieties that are inter-mingled (complanté) in the vineyard. Indeed, floating in the must of the Pinot Noir were several bunches of white grapes. Production here offers both conventional and unconventional wines. The wines are grouped as Vins de Fruits (the usual varieties of Alsace, vinified as single varietals); Vins de Terroirs (wines from specific vineyards, including grand crus: whites consist of various varieties intermingled, and reds consist of Pinot Noir with small amounts of other varieties); and Vins de Temps, which are late harvest wines. Jean-Michel's son Matthieu has been responsible for winemaking since 2008, but Jean-Michel remains in charge, and the philosophy remains as idiosyncratic as ever.

Maison Hugel & Fils **⋆⋆**

📍 3 Rue de La 1ère Armée, 68340 Riquewihr

📞 (33) 03 89 47 92 15

@ info@hugel.com

📇 Etienne Hugel

🌐 www.hugel.com

📷 Alsace

🍾 Les Neveux Jubilee

🍾 Jubilee Riesling

🚶 🏭 G N

30 ha; 1,200,000 bottles

Maison Hugel dates from the seventeenth century and is run by Marc and his cousin Jean-Philippe (the twelfth generation since the house was founded in 1639; Marc's brother Étienne sadly died young in 2016). The winery occupies a picturesque rabbit warren of buildings in the old town of Riquewihr. Hugel is one of the larger negociant-growers, with estate vineyards providing about a quarter of its grapes. There are five lines of wines. Classic (entry level, from purchased grapes), Tradition (mid range, with stricter selection of purchased grapes), and Jubilee (the top cuvées, coming only from estate vineyards) are always fermented dry. This is something Étienne felt strongly about: "It's a very serious problem that affects the whole image of Alsace, with wines being made in sweet styles." Only the late harvest wines, Vendange Tardive and SGN, are sweet. Hugel produces all of the Alsatian varieties, and was a pioneer in introducing Pinot Noir as a serious red wine. Hugel are well known for their rejection of the grand cru system—"The grand cru classification is meaningless as an indication of quality"—so their wines are labeled only as Alsace, although Marc admits, "More than half of our vineyards are in grand crus, and in the best parcels at that, so it's absolutely surreal not to have grand cru on the label." The Jubilee Riesling comes from grand cru Schoenberg, and the Gewürztraminer from Sporen, and they are in fact the defining wines for these appellations.

Domaine Josmeyer ★★

JOSMEYER

ALSACE

PINOT GRIS
GRAND CRU HENGST

 76 Rue Clémenceau, 68920 Wintzen-
heim

☎ (33) 03 89 27 91 90

@ contact@josmeyer.com

👤 Céline Meyer

🌐 www.josmeyer.com

🔲 Alsace

🍷 Les Pierrets, Riesling

🚶 🏭 G 🔖

25 ha; 200,000 bottles

"We make dry white wines to go with food," says Céline Meyer, who runs Domaine Josmeyer together with her sister Isabelle. Created in 1854 by Alois Meyer, the domain is located in charming buildings around a court-yard in typical Alsace style, on the main street. Vineyards are mostly local, but spread out over many small parcels, about 80 in all. Vinification is tra-ditional, with everything matured in old foudres. The focus here is classic: after a quick excursion into Pinot Blanc and Auxerrois (including the Pinot Auxerrois "K" cuvée which comes exclusively from old Auxerrois vines), tasting focuses on Riesling, Pinot Gris, and Gewürztraminer. Going up the range of Rieslings, flavors turn from petrol (in Le Kottabe from the plain) to citrus (in Les Pierrets from the slopes) to stone fruits (in grand crus Brand and Hengst), and the wines become increasingly reserved. These are not wines for instant gratification, but need time for full flavor variety to emerge. In spite of the commitment to dry style, alcohol levels are moder-ate. Brand Riesling is upright and Hengst is more powerful. A similar transition is seen with Pinot Gris, from the classic Fromenteau (Alsace AOP) to Brand and then Hengst: these are as dry as Pinot Gris gets, increasing in richness and power along the range. For Gewürztraminer, Les Folastries is almost dry, and the grand crus are a bit richer. The style brings out varietal character, muddied as little as possible by sugar.

Domaine André Kientzler

🔵 50 route de Bergheim, 68150 Ribeau-villé

📞 (33) 03 89 73 67 10

@ domaine@vinskientzler.com

👤 Eric Kientzler

🌐 http://www.vinskientzler.com/

🔵 Alsace

🔲 G

13 ha; 80,000 bottles

Now in its fifth generation, Kientzler is a highly praised winery, housed in a modern building with a tasting room just off main road outside Ribeauvillé. The coteaux of vineyards rises up opposite. "We look for berries at maturity not surmaturity. We try to make wines that have a dry balance," says Eric Kientzler. Do they always have the same character? "No it is a matter of balance." Fermentation and élevage are in stainless steel, and last up to five months. All of the white varieties are produced, with about 20 cuvées in all. The varietal wines are workmanlike, but where the excitement comes is with the Grand Crus, about a third of the vineyards. The Geisberg Riesling seems to me to me to be far and away the best of Kientzler"s wines.

Domaine Marc Kreydenweiss ★★

⊙ 12, rue Deharbe, 67140 Andlau

📞 (33) 03 88 08 95 83

@ marc@kreydenweiss.com

Marc Kreydenweiss

⊕ www.kreydenweiss.com

▣ Alsace

Wiebelsberg Riesling

14 ha; 70,000 bottles

Located towards the northern tip of the Alsace vineyards, the Kreydenweiss domain was established in the seventeenth century, has been bottling wines since the mid nineteenth century, and includes vineyards that belonged to the Abbaye of Andlau before the French Revolution. The tasting room is located in a charming old house in the village. Marc Kreydenweiss has been running the domain since he took over in 1971 at the age of 23. He was one of the first in Alsace to adopt biodynamic viticulture, and in 1984 decided to focus on single vineyard wines; most of the dozen cuvées come from named plots, culminating in three grand crus. He has expanded beyond Alsace, first by purchasing the Perrières domain near Nîmes in 1999, and then by extending a negociant activity to Châteauneuf-du-Pape. In fact, more wine is now made in the south than at the original estate in Andlau. An unusual feature of vinification here is that malolactic fermentation is encouraged, but this does not seem to detract from the freshness of the wines. The grand cru Rieslings have a penetrating minerality, and the lieu-dit wines follow the same style with less intensity. Pinot Gris often has savory overtones to balance the residual sweetness. Purity is the mark of the house, enhanced by low yields (around 40 hl/ha).

Domaine Albert Mann

ALSACE GRAND CRU
APPELLATION ALSACE GRAND CRU CONTRÔLÉE

GEWURZTRAMINER
GRAND CRU FURSTENTUM
VIEILLES VIGNES 2009

Albert Mann

MIS EN BOUTEILLE AU DOMAINE
ALBERT MANN PROPRIÉTAIRE-VITICULTEUR A 68920 WETTOLSHEIM FRANCE
750 ML   PRODUCE OF FRANCE   ALC. 13.5% BY VOL.

🌐 13 rue du Château, 68920 Wettol-sheim

📞 (33) 03 89 80 62 00

@ vins@albertmann.com

👤 Marie-Claire or Marie-Therese Barthelme

🌐 www.albertmann.com

⬤ Alsace

🍾 Furstentum Pinot Gris

21 ha; 120,000 bottles

The Mann and Barthelmé families have been making wine in Wettolsheim since the 17th century. Albert Mann started bottling his own wine in 1947, and his granddaughter, Marie-Claire, is married to Maurice Barthelmé; since 1989 the domain has included both families' vineyards, and is run today by Maurice together with his brother Jacky and their wives. Five grand crus represent about a third of the hundred vineyard plots. There are about 35 cuvées. Entry-level wines have been bottled under screwcap since 2004; everything else remains under cork. Vinification and aging is in stainless steel, and the wines are bottled relatively early to maintain fresh-ness, except for some cuvées matured in barrique (a Pinot Blanc and the reds). The domain is known for its hands-off approach. "We don't do oe-nology or make technical wine," says Maurice. The entry-level line (Tradition) is fruity and approachable, and mostly off-dry. Rieslings from the lieu-dits and grand crus vary from dry to overtly sweet; Pinot Gris is off-dry or sweet, and Gewürztraminer is always sweet. The three varieties from Furstentum are quintessential. The style is relatively rich and powerful. There's an unusual emphasis on Pinot Noir, with no less than four single vineyard cuvées: Clos de la Faille and Les Saintes Claires from lieu-dits, and Grand P and Grand H from the Pfersigberg and Hengst grand crus.

Meyer Fonné Vins ★★

📍 24 Grand'rue, Katzenthal, 68230
📞 (0)3 89 27 16 50
@ felix@meyer-fonne.com
Felix Meyer
🌐 www.meyer-fonne.com
Alsace
Pfoeller Riesling

15 ha; 85,000 bottles

With a spectacular view from his living room window of the fortress on top of the hill of the Wineck-Schlossberg grand cru, Felix Meyer is right under the vineyards. The Meyer family have been in Katzenthal since 1732; Felix's great grandfather created the domain. The family house is at one end of the courtyard; at the other end are the winery buildings, where everything has been modernized. Felix has been in charge since 1992. He expanded the estate from an initial 6 ha, and now there are vineyards all around the local area, including several grand crus. Riesling and Pinot Blanc are the most important, but all the varieties are made except Sylvaner. There are usually 22-30 cuvées depending on whether there is VT and SGN. The focus is on terroir. "I'm very interested in terroir and passionate about it, we work on five grand crus and three lieu-dits, and this goes back twenty years so it's not something new," Felix says. The first level of wines, Alsace AOP and some Katzenthal village cuvées, are always vinified to dryness, and bottled in the Spring to preserve freshness. The lieu-dits and grand crus usually have a minimal touch of residual sugar, and are bottled just before the next harvest. Felix tries to be consistent. "Each cuvée has a single style, I don't want a cuvée to be sweet one year and dry another year," he says. The Rieslings are quite textured at lower levels and have a tendency to power at the grand cru level. Pinot Gris and Gewürztraminer tend to be quite forceful.

Domaine René Muré ***

◎ Clos Saint Landelin, Route du Vin, RN 83, 68250 Rouffach

📞 (33) 03 89 78 58 01

@ rene@mure.com

👤 Véronique Muré

🌐 www.mure.com

◉ Alsace

🍷 V (Vorbourg)

Riesling Clos St. Landelin

🚶 👑 G N ⌐

25 ha; 150,000 bottles

This family domain has been producing wine since the seventeenth century. Véronique and Thomas Muré, the twelfth generation, work with their father René. In addition to estate vineyards, they buy grapes from growers under long term contract for around another 30 ha. The winery is just south of Rouffach, overlooked by grand cru Vorbourg, which includes the Clos St. Landelin, a monopole that is a lieu-dit at the southern tip purchased by René Muré in 1935. Wines are divided into those under the René Muré label and those under the Clos St. Landelin label, which include grand crus around Rouffach. Vinification is in old foudres (some more than a century old, but with internal temperature control). The wines spend 15 months on the lees. There are all the varieties, with a full range from dry to vendange tardive and SGN, but the Rieslings and Pinot Noirs are the signature wines here. Crémant and brandy are produced as well as still wine. Pinot Noir is about 10% of production, and has increased in proportion with the recent run of warm vintages (a return to the past as Rouffach was known for red wines in the Middle Ages). "Clos St. Landelin, it's paradise for Pinot Noir," says René. Wines under the René Muré label are intended for consumption relatively soon, but those under the St. Landelin label should have longevity of one to two decades. Riesling is intense and racy; Pinot Noir is earthy and spicy.

Domaine Ostertag ★★

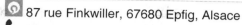 87 rue Finkwiller, 67680 Epfig, Alsace

📞 (33) 03 88 85 51 34

@ domaine-ostertag@wanadoo.fr

👤 Andre Ostertag

🌐 domaine-ostertag.fr

Alsace

🍷 Muenchberg, Pinot Gris

14 ha; 100,000 bottles

This domain was created by André's father in 1966, but he abruptly handed over the winemaking in 1980 to André when he was only twenty. There's more freedom to innovate here than in a domain bound by a long history. Behind the unassuming front on a back street in Epfig is a charming courtyard, surrounded by winery buildings. André essentially works the domain alone, using only estate grapes from his 75 individual vineyard plots. "This is crucial because the major part of quality comes from the work in the vineyards," André says. There are three series of wines: the basic series are AOP Alsace, there are some grand crus, and then there are the Vendange Tardive or SGNs. Except for the latter and for the Gewürztraminer, all the wines are dry. The Pinot Blanc is matured in barrique and (unusually for Alsace) goes through malolactic fermentation. In fact, the grand crus are sometimes refused the agrément on grounds of lack of typicity (because of exposure to new oak), and a compromise has been reached in which the name of the grand cru is put on the back label rather than stated on the front. About 7-8% of production is Pinot Noir, which also is matured in barriques rather than the traditional foudres. There is 100% destemming to make the wine as soft as possible, and délestage (a procedure in which the must is racked off and pumped back) is used rather than pigeage. The village wine uses one third oak and is bottled in July.

Domaine Schlumberger

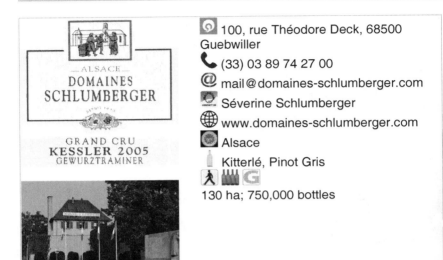

🌀 100, rue Théodore Deck, 68500 Guebwiller

📞 (33) 03 89 74 27 00

@ mail@domaines-schlumberger.com

👤 Séverine Schlumberger

🌐 www.domaines-schlumberger.com

◉ Alsace

🍾 Kitterlé, Pinot Gris

130 ha; 750,000 bottles

Schlumberger's vineyards are in a long contiguous block running along the hillside (really more like a mountain slope) parallel with the town of Guebwiller, which nestles under the mountain. Vineyards are mostly at elevations of 250-350 m. To visit the vineyards, Séverine Schlumberger drives you up from the town in a Landrover. As the road goes up from the town, it narrows into little more than a muddy path running along a ledge between successive terraces of vineyards, with a sheer drop to the vineyards below. At one point it becomes so narrow that you are asked to get out and walk ahead while the car inches along behind, rather than risk everyone in the Landrover. It's around this point, Severine says with a wicked grin, that they usually ask clients if they'd like to complete the order form. Established with Nicolas Schlumberger's purchase of 20 ha in 1810, today Schlumberger is one of the larger landholders in Alsace, with half of the holdings in the four grand crus around Guebwiller. "We don't believe in following fashions, which come and go, but make very much the same mix of varieties and styles as traditionally," Séverine says. Vinification is in foudres of very old oak. The wines are divided into Les Princes Abbés (with all seven of the varieties), the Grand Crus (with Riesling, Pinot Gris, and Gewürztraminer), and Les Collections (Vendange Tardive or SGN dessert wines). All wines come exclusively from the estate, and are very reliable.

Domaine Schoffit

66-68 Nonnenholzweg par Rue-des-Aubepines, 68000 Colmar

(33) 03 89 24 41 14

domaine.schofit@free.fr

Alexandre Schoffit

Alsace

Rangen, Clos St. Théobald Riesling

16 ha; 120,000 bottles

The domain has an obscure location at the end of a tiny road through a housing estate close to the autoroute on the eastern edge of Colmar, yet there is a constant stream of visitors to the tasting room. Vineyards extend from Colmar to the south. The most important are in grand cru Rangen (well to the south at the end of the grand crus). There are all the cépages of Alsace, with a majority of Riesling. Depending on the year, there are 20-30 cuvées. Fermentation is allowed to proceed until it stops naturally, which usually leaves around 6 g/l residual sugar for Riesling, 7 g/l for Pinot Blanc, 12 g/l for Pinot Gris, and 30 g/l for Gewürztraminer. In the introductory range, Tradition, the wines taste drier than in the Caroline range, which is richer. Cuvée Alexandre is used for wines that are sweet but not labeled as Vendange Tardive. Wines from lieu-dit Harth have more concentration than AOP Alsace, and grand cru Sommerberg (only available in small amounts for old clients) increases in complexity; the top of the range is Rangen and the wines from the Clos St. Théobald monopole within it. For Riesling, Sommerberg showcases tense acidity and Rangen brings out delicacy. The Gewurztraminers are unusually subtle at levels ranging from sweet through VT to SGN. Vendange Tardive for both Pinot Gris and Gewurztraminer shows its character more as texture and flavor variety than overt sweetness; lovely if you want the flavor spectrum without too much sweetness.

Maison Louis Sipp

5 Grand'rue, 68150 Ribeauvillé

(33) 03 89 73 60 01

Louis@Sipp.Com

Etienne Sipp

www.sipp.com

Alsace

Osterberg Riesling

40 ha; 350,000 bottles

In charge of this family domain since 1996, Etienne Sipp has a thoughtful, quasi-academic approach, perhaps explained by his Ph.D. in mineral science. Created after the first world war, the domain has been located right in the center of picturesque Ribeauvillé since 1933. Today production comes exclusively from estate grapes, "From the historical part of the vineyards on the slopes," Etienne says. "Our vineyards are concentrated in a radius of 3-4 km," he adds, explaining that this is an area within a fractal field that is exceptionally diverse in its soil types. "Geology and climate are very specific here, which is why we can produce a high diversity of wines. The only negative is that the wines do not open quickly; they age well but need some time to open." Under a yellow label, the entry level range is divided into young wines and Nature'S wines, the latter being organic; the Reserve Personelle wines have longer aging before release. There are five single vineyards and two grand crus in the cuvées from specific terroirs, as well, of course, as late harvest. Purity of style allow vintage influence to show directly, as illustrated by a vertical of Riesling from Osterberg: 2010 is steely citrus, austere and needing time; 2009 is soft pleasure, with a smile of sweetness on the stewed citrus; 2008 is all delicate citrus; 2007 is more reserved; 2004 is quite floral. Pinot Gris and Gewürztraminer are more forward, and here the reserved style can translate into delicacy.

Maison Pierre Sparr & Fils

2 Rue de La 1ère Armée Française, 68240 Sigolsheim

(33) 03 89 78 24 22

@ info@vins-sparr.com

Vincent Lallier

www.vins-sparr.com

Alsace

130 ha; 800,000 bottles

This old negociant has a complicated history that led to decline. It was divided between two brothers, each had two sons, and in 2007 there was a split; one side of the family left, the rest remained. (There"s still a Sparr making wines but he isn"t allowed to use the name,) The negociant went into bankruptcy and was bought by the cooperative at Beblenheim in 2009. Today Sparr owns 15 ha and buys grapes from 240 ha. Some of the growers are very small, so there are some cuvées from amalgamating lots from several grand crus based on commonality of terroir. There is no distinction on the label between estate and purchased grapes. The scale of production is large: "too many tocount," is the answer when you ask how many cuvées there are. Headquarters is a rather commercial looking establishment in Sigolsheim . Grand Reserve is the entry level wine. It"s under cork for France and Belgium, screwcaps elsewhere. Vincent Lallier came as winemaker in 2007 to modernize production, focus more on fruit, protect against oxidation, and use longer élevage on the lees. It"s fair to say that there are real efforts at improving quality, but you have to go to the grand cru level to see it. The best wine to my mind is the atypically austere Mambourg grand cru Riesling. Grand cru Altenbourg or the terroir-based Alsace Sol Granitique are more typical, with disernable residual sugar.

Marc Tempé

 16 rue Schlossberg, 68340 Zellenberg

📞 (33) 06 08 05 40 32

@ contact@lasommeliere.fr

 Marc Tempé

⊕ www.marctempe.fr

 Alsace

🍾 Grafenreben Riesling

8 ha; 40,000 bottles

Located in an old house in the square in Zellenberg, the domain looks like it might go back eons, but in fact was started by Anne-Marie and Marc Tempé in 1993 when they obtained vineyards from their parents, who were retiring as members of the cooperative. "We asked ourselves what we should do with 7 ha, we had a clean slate, we weren't obliged to follow the history of our parents and grandparents. It was obvious to me that I should make wine as I wanted," says Marc. The domain remains small and hands-on: Marc came back from the vineyards on his tractor for our tasting. The clean slate has led to a distinctive style in which the wines have long élevage in barriques. "My aim is to make a dry wine because it goes best with food. Fermentation is never stopped here because the wine stays two years in cave with no intervention. It will find an equilibrium even if sometimes there is residual sugar," explains Marc. So some of the wines have a minimal level of sugar, just at the level of detection, but perfectly integrated. The wines are flavorful, with Rieslings generally soft but delicate, yet conveying a definite sense of silky texture. Pinot Gris shows its character with a herbal texture, and Gewürztraminer conveys an unusual sense of varietal character without becoming overwhelming. The Vendange Tardive or SGN Gewürztraminer is a knockout for its delicacy. In fact, if a single word describes the domain it's that delicacy of character running through the range.

Maison Trimbach   **

15 route de Bergheim, 68150 Ribeau-villé, Alsace

(33) 03 89 73 60 30

@ contact@maison-trimbach.fr

Pierre Trimbach

www.maison-trimbach.fr

Alsace

Frédéric Emile Riesling

45 ha; 1,300,000 bottles

One of the most important houses in Alsace, Trimbach remains a hands-on family business. "I can still drive a fork lift when needed," says Pierre Trimbach. Trimbach's heart is in Riesling, which is more than half of production. Riesling is always completely dry, and Pinot Gris and Gewürztraminer are vinified as dry as balance will allow. The winery on the main road through Ribeauvillé has a quaint appearance—Trimbach goes back to 1626—but wine production is entirely modern. Trimbach owns enough vineyards to supply about a third of its grapes. The Trimbachs do not believe in the grand cru system, although the wines for their top Rieslings come from grand cru terroir, Frédéric Emile from 6 ha in Geisberg and Osterberg, and Clos St. Hune from 1.67 ha in Rosacker. Recently, they have in fact introduced the first grand cru, a Geisberg Riesling. Yellow labels identify the Classic and Réserve lines. Gold labels indicate the terroir wines, which include Frédéric Emile Riesling, Réserve Personelle Pinot Gris, and Seigneurs de Ribeaupierre Gewürztraminer. White labels are the very peak, including Clos St. Hune and the Vendange Tardive and SGN. The style of Riesling is mineral, saline, bordering on austerity; going up the hierarchy, increasing time is needed for development, a couple of years for Réserve, five years for Geisberg (which is richer than Frédéric Emile), eight for Frédéric Emile, and at least a dozen for Clos St. Hune, which is widely acknowledged as one of the top Rieslings of Alsace.

44

Domaine Weinbach   ***

🔘 25 route route du Vin, 68240 Kientz-heim

📞 (33) 03 89 47 13 21

@ contact@domaineweinbach.com

📇 Catherine Faller

🌐 www.domaineweinbach.com

🔵 Alsace

🍾 Riesling Schlossberg, Cuvée St. Catherine

🚶 🍾 G 〰️

30 ha; 120,000 bottles

This matriarchal domain makes some of the most precise and elegant wines in Alsace. It really doesn't matter if the variety is Riesling, Gewürztraminer or Pinot Noir: there is always that precise delineation of flavors. The name on the label says Domaine Weinbach, but the wall surrounding the Clos de Capucines at the heart of the vineyard (underneath the hill of grand cru Schlossberg) says Domaine Faller on one side and Le Weinbach (the name of the lieu-dit) on the other. The domain was acquired in 1898 by the Faller brothers, inherited by Théo Faller, and since 1979 run by his wife, Colette, and her daughters Catherine and Laurence. All the varieties are produced, and the wines are vinified dry with some notable exceptions. Where else do you find such elegant Muscat or refined Gewürztraminer, let alone the granular Pinot Gris and the steely Rieslings? The Rieslings are certainly the top of the line, from cuvée Théo (from the Clos des Capucines), Schlossberg, Cuvée Sainte Catherine (from the oldest parcels at the foot of Schlossberg), and Sainte Catherine l'Inédit, which comes from the best parcels in Schlossberg in the best years, and is the exception that often has a touch of residual sugar. There's a similar range of Pinot Gris and Gewürztraminer, and a brilliant Pinot Noir. 2014 was a sad year for the domain because Laurence, the talented young winemaker, died unexpectedly in May, followed later by Colette. Catherine and her family continue.

Domaine Zind Humbrecht ★★★

⊙ 4 route de Colmar, BP 22, 68230 Turckheim

☎ (33) 03 89 27 02 05

@ o.humbrecht@zind-humbrecht.fr

👤 Olivier Humbrecht

🌐 www.zindhumbrecht.fr

◉ Alsace

🍾 Herrenweg de Turckheim Riesling

🚶 🏭 G ⟋

40 ha; 200,000 bottles

Created in 1959 with the marriage of Léonard Humbrecht to Geneviève Zind, this domain has become one of the best regarded in Alsace under the leadership of their son Olivier, who took over in 1989. Humbrechts have been making wine here since the seventeenth century. The domain moved to a stylish new building in the Herrenberg vineyard in 1992. Zind-Humbrecht was a pioneer in biodynamic viticulture and in reducing yields, typically now around 30-40 hl/ha. One consequence is increased richness, which is allowed to show itself by levels of residual sugar that vary with the vintage; the domain was one of the first (in 2001) to indicate the level of sweetness by marking it on the label against a five point scale. Most wines are bottled as lieu-dits, so there are around 30 cuvées altogether. The best known are perhaps Clos Windsbuhl (close to the Rosacker grand cru) and Clos Saint Urbain (a monopole within the Rangen grand cru). The only generic wines are Zind (a Chardonnay-Auxerrois blend from Windsbuhl labeled as Vin de France), Pinot Blanc, Riesling, and Muscat. The Calcaire cuvées come from calcareous terroirs. Then there are 7 Rieslings from lieu-dits or grand crus, 4 Pinot Gris, and 4 Gewürztraminers as well as the vendange tardive and SGN. The hands-off approach makes it hard to find a single description for the style, but it tends to a rich and powerful expression of each variety. Olivier is sceptical about Pinot Noir, so the emphasis remains on whites.

Domaine Valentin Zusslin ✶✶

ALSACE

RIESLING
Clos Liebenberg 2000
Grande Réserve

📍 57 Grand'rue, 68500 Orschwihr
📞 (33) 03 89 76 82 84
@ info@zusslin.com
👤 Marie & Jean Paul Zusslin
🌐 www.zusslin.com
Alsace
Bollenberg Harmonie
Clos Liebenberg Riesling
16 ha; 90,000 bottles

Jean-Paul and his sister Marie are the thirteenth generation to run this family domain since the Zusslins moved from Switzerland three centuries ago to settle in Orschwihr, where there are now several producers called Zusslin in the Grand'Rue. Their history is emphasized by a huge genealogical chart on the wall of the tasting room. Riesling is the most important variety, but unusually Pinot Noir is close behind. The main three cuvées are the Rieslings from Bollenberg (a lieu-dit), Clos Liebenberg (a monopole close to grand cru Pfingstberg), and Pfingstberg. Rieslings are pressed slowly for 10-12 hours, settled, and fermented in foudres. The style is racy, a very pure and precise expression of the variety, with intensity and savory overtones increasing from Bollenberg to Clos Liebenberg to Pfingstberg. A vertical of Pfingstberg similarly shows savory elements increasing with age and beginning to turn tertiary after ten years. The Bollenberg Harmonie Pinot Noir (Harmonie is the best plot for reds in Bollenberg) offers smooth red fruits supported by silky tannins and lovely aromatics. It's destemmed, vinified in wooden cuves, and matured in barriques with 50% new oak. The impression is softer and more aromatic than Burgundy, but very fine. About five years after the vintage is the right time to start the reds. In some years there is a vendange tardive Riesling from Pfingstberg, which is extraordinarily subtle; in fact, subtle is the one word that sums up the domain.

Index of Estates by Rating

Zusslin 2013 Brut Zero
Cremant d' Alsace

Rolly Gassmann
Riesling Alsace
Rorschwihr Selection de
Grains Nobles 2010

Index of Estates by Name

INTELLIGENT GUIDES TO WINES & TOP VINEYARDS

WINES OF FRANCE SERIES

Bordeaux: Left Bank
Bordeaux: Right Bank
Southwest France
Burgundy: Chablis & Côte d'Or
Southern Burgundy, Beaujolais & Jura
Champagne
Alsace
The Loire
The Rhône
Languedoc
Provence and Corsica

WINE OF EUROPE SERIES

Barolo & Barbaresco
Tuscany
Port & the Douro

NEW WORLD WINE SERIES

Napa Valley & Sonoma

BOOKS by Benjamin Lewin MW

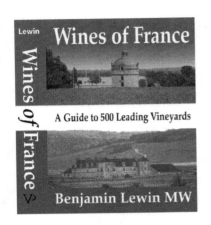

Wines of France

This comprehensive account of the vineyards and wines of France today is extensively illustrated with photographs and maps of each wine-producing area. Leading vineyards and winemakers are profiled in detail, with suggestions for wines to try and vineyards to visit.

Claret & Cabs:
the Story of Cabernet Sauvignon

This worldwide survey of Cabernet Sauvignon and its blends extends from Bordeaux through the New World, defines the character of the wine from each region, and profiles leading producers.

In Search of Pinot Noir

Pinot Noir is a uniquely challenging grape with an unrivalled ability to reflect the character of the site where it grows. This world wide survey of everywhere Pinot Noir is grown extends from Burgundy to the New World, and profiles leading producers.

Wine Myths and Reality

Extensively illustrated with photographs, maps, and charts, this behind-the-scenes view of winemaking reveals the truth about what goes into a bottle of wine. Its approachable and entertaining style immediately engages the reader in the wine universe.

What Price Bordeaux?

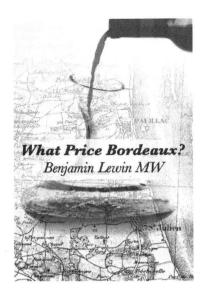

A revolution is underway in Bordeaux. Top chateaux have been obtaining unprecedented prices for their wines, while smaller chateaux are going bankrupt. Extending from the changing character of Bordeaux wines to market forces, this unique overview reveals the forces making Bordeaux wine what it is today.

About the Author

Benjamin Lewin MW brings a unique combination of qualifications in wine and science to bear on the world of wine. He is one of only 300 Masters of Wine, and was the founding Editor of *Cell* journal. His previous books received worldwide critical acclaim for their innovative approach. Lewin also writes the myths and realities column in the *World of Fine Wine*, and contributes to *Decanter* magazine, *Wine & Spirits*, among others. His blog on wine is at *www.lewinonwine.com*. He divides his time between the eastern United States and the wine-growing regions of Europe, and is presently working on his next book.

37525172R00036

Made in the USA
Middletown, DE
30 November 2016